Myths
of the Sea

Contents

Seán and the Sea-Maiden

Written by Malachy Doyle

Illustrated by Gary Cherrington

Part 1

Seán was down by the shore one day when he heard a joyful song:

I'm a maiden of the sea,
and I'm swimming, yes, I'm swimming.
I'm a maiden of the sea,
and I'm swimming to the shore.

Seán hid behind a rock and watched as a sea-maiden came to land, peeled off her shining sea-skin, and raced up and down the beach – still singing her happy song:

I'm a maiden of the sea,
and I'm kicking up the sand!

While she was up at the other end of the beach, Seán ran out from behind his rock, grabbed her sea-skin, and hid it under an old broken rowing boat.

At the end of her song, the sea-maiden returned to where she had left her sea-skin. "Oh, woe is me!" she cried.

"What's the matter?" asked Seán, coming out from behind the rock.

"I've lost my sea-skin!" sobbed the girl. "How can I go home to my family beneath the ocean?"

"You can come home with me," said Seán, who lived with his grandmother.

So the sea-maiden had no choice but to go back with the boy to his granny's cottage, where the old woman gave her clothes to wear, food to eat and a bed to lie in.

Seán was happy, for he was the only child on the island, and he'd found himself a friend at last.

Seán and the sea-maiden became the very best of friends. They built sandcastles on the beach, they played with the boy's little dog, Sandy, and they watched the birds fly, the clouds scudding through the sky, and the waves come crashing to shore.

The sea-maiden, though, never set foot in or on the mighty ocean, for fear that without her sea-skin she might drown. Seán also stayed away from the sea. For although he loved to swim in the water and sail his little green boat around the island, he feared that it might make the girl think of her home, beneath the waves.

In fact, she rarely thought about anything else. Every morning, while Seán was still sleeping, the sea-maiden went down to the shore and sang the saddest song:

I want to go home
to my friends and my family,
I want to go home to the sea.

She knew that it was hopeless, though – for without her sea-skin she was trapped on the island.

Part 2

Early one morning, while the sea-maiden was down on the beach, there came a sudden flash of lightning, a ferocious thunderclap, and rain pelted down from the clouds above.

The girl, searching for shelter, tried to crawl in under an old broken rowing boat – and there she saw … her sea-skin! With a cry of joy, she pulled it on and raced to the water.

"Stop!" cried Seán, who had come to rescue her from the storm. "Don't leave me!"

"But I've found my sea-skin!" yelled the girl. "At last I can go home to my friends and family!"

"This is your home now," said Seán, "and I am your brother."

"No," said the sea-maiden, shaking her head. "You've been a good friend to me, Seán, but my real life is in the sea, and everyone there will be missing me sorely."

She broke into joyful song:

I'm coming on home
to my people at last.
Oh, I'm coming on home to the sea!

Then she ran to the ocean and was gone.

Seán was sad to have lost his only friend, but he returned to the life he'd had before she arrived. At least he was able to go back out on the water again, now that the sea-maiden had gone.

One day though, another storm blew up while he was out checking his lobster pots. Seán's boat was blown out to sea and the waves got bigger and bigger, till the young fisher-boy didn't know which way was home, and till the last of his strength was fading.

"Help!" he yelled, over the howling of the wind and the crashing of the waves. "Somebody help me!"

So far from land, there was no one to help. No one to hear.

Suddenly, there was the sea-maiden in the water beside him.

"Don't worry, Seán," she cried. "We'll guide you back to shore!"

She called up her friends and family, and together they led him through the waves and all the way back to his island.

"Oh, thank you," gasped Seán, pulling the boat from the water. "I don't know what I would have done if you hadn't come to help me."

"That's all right," replied the sea-maiden. "You and your granny were kind to me, while I was stranded on your island, so I will always watch out for you while you are at sea."

She swam away, singing happily:

I'm a maiden of the sea,
and I'll guide you, yes, I'll guard you.
I'm a maiden of the sea,
and I'll always keep you safe.

So Seán and the sea-maiden often met up, out at sea. They met while he was ashore too, for sometimes, when the boy was sitting on the rocks or walking the beach, she'd come in close, to chat and to sing.

They stayed the best of friends but the sea-maiden never came ashore again.

And, though they talked about anything and everything, the sea-maiden never asked how her sea-skin had come to be tucked in under the little old rowing boat.

And Seán never said.

Odysseus and the Monster

Written by Nikki Tate
Illustrated by Galia Bernstein

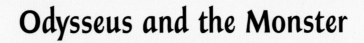

Part 1

Odysseus and his crew are sailing home from war, but their troubles are not over. The sea journey is full of dangers …

We were all relieved when our ship entered a stretch of water that was sheltered by cliffs and the wind died. Whatever hopes we may have had for a gentle day at sea were dashed, though, when Odysseus shouted at us. "Take up the oars, men! Pull as hard as you can! We must pass by this evil place as fast as possible."

Standing at his usual place at the front, Odysseus watched the sea. A deep BOOM rang out from the cliffs on our left side. Smoke rose up as if a great fire burned on the sea itself. Waves whipped around in an ever-tightening circle, sucking everything in reach down into a long black tunnel beneath the sea. The waters around the whirlpool churned and boiled and the waves rose and crashed against the jagged rocks beyond.

Odysseus spoke to the man steering us.
"Stay clear of that whirlpool!
Terrible danger awaits us if we
come too close to Charybdis."
To the rest of us he said,
"Row hard. Passing
through here at speed
is our only chance
of reaching
safety. We
must not be
sucked down
Charybdis's
throat or
we shall
perish."

Our captain then looked in the opposite direction, across the strait to a wall of dark cliffs rising up out of the sea to our right. His mouth opened as if to speak, but he said nothing.

When I looked up again, he was wearing his polished armour and wielding not one, but two long spears. I had no time to wonder what horrors awaited us. A movement at the mouth of a cave high in the cliff face above us caught my eye. I clutched at my oar, my knuckles white and fingers aching. My heart thudded with the effort of pulling against the waves.

Dreadful whimpering cries came from somewhere beyond the black slit of the cave opening. The sound was that of misery itself. Something poked out from deep inside the cave. It was a ghastly head on a neck that stretched so far away from the cliff that I thought, at first, it was a massive kite. It was followed by another head and then another, each more hideous than the one before. Each gaping mouth had three rows of jagged teeth, sharp as broken glass. Six heads at the ends of impossibly long necks strained to reach away from the cliff, sharp eyes scanning the sea for a good meal.

"What is that?" I asked.

"Scylla," Odysseus replied, raising both his spears as if they might protect us all from the monster's attack.

One of the heads snapped at a seal sunning itself on a rock. The creature flung itself into the sea, saved by its quick reflexes. Scylla snarled and gnashed her teeth.

Every muscle of my back, my legs, my arms ached and shook but I dared not stop rowing.

Part 2

On the far shore, Charybdis, the violent whirlpool, gulped down anything that floated past. Moments later, she spat forth plumes of black stinking spray that rose high into the air. What a dreadful choice Odysseus had to make: the unforgiving whirlpool on one side; Scylla's gobbling heads on the other.

Odysseus looked from one to the other and then raised his spears and pointed dead ahead, a course that would take us along the foot of Scylla's cliff home. Not a sound was to be heard from any of us except for our desperate heavy breathing.

"Faster!" Odysseus cried out
and exhausted though we were, we
gripped our oars more tightly.

As one, all six of Scylla's heads
turned and fixed their gaze upon our
ship. Like snakes they struck, one and then
another, clamping those terrible teeth around
six of the men. I threw myself sideways and dived
as low in the boat as I could. The monster's breath was
hot and steamy against my arm. I choked back a scream and
pressed myself against the deck.

As if they were no heavier than small fish, Scylla plucked
the six sailors from where they sat and hauled them back up
to her cave. The men's arms and legs flailed wildly and they
cried out, "Save us! Odysseus!"

He raised his weapons and stabbed at the closest head. The tip of one spear was knocked aside. The other pierced the monster's bottom lip and she roared. Though Odysseus fought bravely, lunging and stabbing, leaping as high as he could to try to spear the monster and free his men, Scylla did not let go. As Scylla retreated, Odysseus threw his spears after her, but they tumbled uselessly into the sea.

"To your oars!" Odysseus shouted. I began to row once more. Though six of our strongest men were gone, our ship moved faster than it ever had. We all knew that if Scylla was still hungry, any one of us might be her next course.

When we were far enough past the cliffs that we could rest a moment, I asked, "Did you know what lurked in that cave?"

Odysseus turned his back to me and gazed out across the open ocean. After a long pause he said, "To lose six men is a terrible thing, but to lose the ship and all those aboard would have been far worse." His voice was steady, but his shoulders slumped and he sighed deeply before adding, "Best we not think of what has passed. We have a long way to go."

Without argument, we took hold of our oars, eager to reach land and find somewhere to rest.

Real Sea Monsters

Written by Holly Bennett

Legend Come to Life?

The legend of the Kraken describes a huge, tentacled creature big enough to destroy a ship. The Kraken isn't real, but there *is* a real animal that may have inspired the legend. The giant squid can grow 12 metres long or more, and weigh up to 900 kilograms. With eight thick arms lined with toothed suckers, two feeding tentacles that can shoot out and snatch prey, and a sharp beak for slicing up its meal, this squid is well armed!

From Giant to Colossal

Not big enough for you? The colossal squid is even bigger! We don't know much about this rare squid, because very few people have seen or caught one.

DID YOU KNOW?

These huge squid have the biggest eyes on Earth. Their eyes grow up to 25 centimetres across — that's an eyeball the size of a human head!

Jellyfish Giants

If you've been to the beach, you may have seen jellyfish washed up on shore or floating in the water. If you've had the bad luck to get stung, you'll know that it can hurt – so imagine a jellyfish over two metres across with over 800 stinging tentacles trailing 30 metres behind it! That's how big a Lion's Mane jellyfish can grow. The big ones are rare, and live in deep, cold, Arctic waters.

How They Hunt

The Lion's Mane jellyfish hunts just by floating down through the ocean. Its long, stringy tentacles spread out around it like a huge net. Each tentacle is lined with hundreds of special cells called nematocysts. When these cells are touched, they fire out a barbed thread like a tiny harpoon that injects venom into its prey.

How Big Are They?

It's hard to picture just how long these creatures are. Why not get a tape measure and mark out their size on the school playground?

What Should You Do?

Nematocysts can sting even after the jellyfish dies – so never touch one that you find on the beach!

Published by Pearson Education Limited, 80 Strand, London, WC2R 0RL.

www.pearsonschools.co.uk

Text © Pearson Education Limited 2016
Designed by Bigtop Design Ltd

Original illustrations © Pearson Education Limited 2016
Illustrated by Gary Cherrington and Galia Bernstein

First published 2016

20 19 18 17 16
10 9 8 7 6 5 4 3 2

British Library Cataloguing in Publication Data
A catalogue record for this book is available from the British Library

ISBN 978 0 435 18052 2

Printed in China by Golden Cup

Acknowledgements
The publisher would like to thank the following individuals and organisations for
their kind permission to reproduce photographs:

(Key: b-bottom; c-centre; l-left; r-right; t-top)

Alamy Images: Mary Evans Picture Library 22tr, Waterframe 23c;
Science Photo Library Ltd: Christian Darkin 22bl

Cover Front: Science Photo Library Ltd: Christian Darkin

All other images © Pearson Education